CW01512579

Original title:
Harmonious Horizons

Author: Paula Raudsepp
ISBN HARDBACK: 978-1-80560-081-7
ISBN PAPERBACK: 978-1-80560-546-1

Songs of the Weaving Sky

Above the trees, the colors blend,
A tapestry where dreams ascend.
Threads of gold and shades of blue,
Whisper secrets to the dew.

Clouds drift softly, tales unfold,
Stories from the days of old.
In each pattern, life is spun,
A dance of shadows, light, and sun.

Stars ignite in twilight's grace,
A celestial, endless space.
Each twinkle sings a lonesome tune,
Bathing night in soft, silver moon.

The winds carry the notes of time,
Rustling leaves in silent rhyme.
With every gust, a promise flies,
In the songs of the weaving skies.

So let us gaze as colors swirl,
In the canvas of this world.
Find our peace in shades of light,
Underneath the starry night.

Solace Found at the Horizon's Edge

Where the sea meets the twilight glow,
Gentle waves in a quiet flow.
Footprints linger on golden sand,
A map of dreams where we took a stand.

Beneath the sky, in hues of flame,
Whispers call us, soft and tame.
The horizon stretches, wide and free,
Holding secrets, whispered glee.

Clouds drift slowly, painting the skies,
Reflecting hopes, our shared sighs.
The sun dips low, a final bow,
In this moment, we make our vow.

Stars awaken, one by one,
The day is finished, night begun.
In the stillness, we find our way,
Solace found as colors sway.

Together here, on nature's stage,
We turn each chapter, page by page.
In this space, our hearts align,
At the horizon's edge, you are mine.

Unity Beyond the Blue

In the sky so wide and free,
We find hope between the clouds.
Hearts beat in harmony,
United, we stand proud.

Spirit whispers through the air,
Binding souls, both near and far.
In our laughter, we declare,
Together, we are a star.

Through the storms and sunlit days,
We weave dreams in gentle threads.
In every word, in every gaze,
Connection in all that spreads.

Beneath the vast and endless dome,
We are one with every hue.
The world becomes our cherished home,
In love, we find what is true.

From the mountains to the seas,
We shall rise, never to fall.
With the strength of ancient trees,
In unity, we stand tall.

When Stars Align in Silence

In quiet moments, we can see,
The magic in the night unfold.
Twinkling lights like memory,
Whispers of secrets untold.

A cosmic dance in tranquil grace,
Time stops, and breaths entwine.
Underneath the vast embrace,
Our hopes and dreams align.

The universe in its repose,
Guides our hearts to where we long.
In the stillness, passion grows,
Echoing our silent song.

Every star a story shared,
Woven threads of fate and chance.
In the night, we feel unscared,
Carried deep in love's sweet dance.

When tomorrow breaks the night,
Memories of starlit smiles.
In the dawn, we find our light,
Guided by celestial miles.

Symphony of the Waking World

Morning breaks with softest sound,
Birds join in a sweet refrain.
Nature's chorus, all around,
Gentle drops of golden rain.

Each leaf rustles, whispers low,
Stories from the night before.
With every breeze, the colors flow,
Awakening the heart's core.

Sunlight dances on the stream,
Casting sparkles, bright and clear.
In this moment, we can dream,
Embracing all that we hold dear.

Flowers bloom in radiant hues,
Painting earth with vibrant grace.
In their beauty, we choose,
To find joy in every space.

Together, we will roam this land,
In harmony, our spirits soar.
With nature's symphony so grand,
We awaken, craving more.

Embrace of the Endless Dawn

As night falls, it whispers peace,
A promise of the light to come.
In shadows, we find our release,
Awakening to a new drum.

The horizon blushes in gold,
A canvas of dreams yet to chase.
With every moment, we are bold,
Ready to embrace this space.

The morning mist begins to rise,
Kissing earth with tender grace.
Within our hearts, hope always lies,
Radiance in every trace.

In this dawn, we find our song,
A melody soft as the breeze.
With every note, we all belong,
In the cycle, we find ease.

As the day unfolds its face,
We walk together, hand in hand.
In the warmth of this embrace,
Our spirits merge, forever planned.

The Dawn's Gentle Caress

The sun peeks over the hill,
Awakening dreams, soft and still.
Whispers of morning fill the air,
A tender light, a loving care.

Birds sing sweet songs in the trees,
A melody danced by the breeze.
Golden rays kiss the dew,
Nature awakens, fresh and new.

Shadows retreat from the light,
Colors bloom, igniting the sight.
The world stirs from slumbered rest,
In dawn's embrace, we are blessed.

Hope rises with the sun anew,
A canvas painted in vibrant hue.
With every step, a promise grows,
In the dawn's gentle caress, love flows.

Boundless Skies of Reflection

Endless azure stretches wide,
A perfect stage where dreams abide.
Clouds wander, free and high,
Painting tales across the sky.

Mirrors of calm in the deep,
Where thoughts and stars softly leap.
Beneath this vast, uncharted space,
We find ourselves in endless grace.

Time drifts lightly on each breeze,
Horizons painted with quiet ease.
In stillness, echoes softly ring,
Boundless skies, our hearts take wing.

Each moment a glimpse, each thought a ray,
In the sky's embrace, we lose our way.
Reflections linger, bright and wide,
In the celestial dance, we confide.

Colors in the Garden of Dreams

Petals unfurl in soft embrace,
Whispers of color, a gentle grace.
In the garden where hopes ignite,
Every bloom tells a story bright.

Roses blush in shades of red,
Tulips bow, their dreams widespread.
Lilies sway with secrets rare,
In this haven, joy fills the air.

Butterflies flit from flower to flower,
In this symphony, beauty will tower.
Each hue a promise, each scent a song,
In the garden of dreams, we all belong.

Sunlight spills like liquid gold,
Every corner, a tale unfolds.
In the richness of life, we find our way,
Colors bloom anew with each passing day.

Sublime Silhouettes at Twilight

Shadows stretch on the fading light,
Silhouettes dance in the coming night.
Whispers of stars begin to gleam,
In the twilight, we chase a dream.

The horizon melts in hues of blue,
Embers of day bid their adieu.
Softly the world begins to sigh,
As mystery cloaks the evening sky.

Each silhouette tells a story untold,
In the gentle dusk, our hearts unfold.
Beneath the stars, our secrets weave,
In the twilight's embrace, we believe.

The moon rises high, a watchful eye,
In its glow, our thoughts can fly.
Sublime moments captured in time,
At twilight, life feels like a rhyme.

Colors of a Blooming Dawn

The sky awakens with tender hues,
Blushing pink and whispers of blue.
Sunlight dances on petals fair,
Nature's canvas, beyond compare.

Morning brews in fragrant air,
Each color sings of sweet affair.
Dewdrops glisten like tiny stars,
A masterpiece that heals all scars.

Gold spills forth on silken fields,
With every ray, new beauty yields.
Horizon blushes, life anew,
Colors merge in a lovely view.

Birds lift songs, an early choir,
Painting dreams with wings of fire.
As twilight fades into the past,
Hope is born, bright and steadfast.

Embrace the dawn, so soft, so kind,
Let its colors fill your mind.
In every shade, a story found,
In every bloom, love's echo resounds.

Choreography of Light and Shade

Shadows waltz on the cobbled stone,
As the sun dips low, they are not alone.
Figures flicker in the fading rays,
Crafting magic in twilight's maze.

Ballet of light on the forest floor,
Whispers secrets from the ancient lore.
Leaves flutter gently, casting spells,
Nature's rhythm, where wonder dwells.

Refracted beams weave tales of old,
Tales of warmth, in winter's hold.
Light glistens where darkness crept,
In each fold, a promise kept.

Silhouettes dance, graceful and free,
Painting moments for you and me.
In the interplay, life finds its tune,
Under the watch of the glowing moon.

As day surrenders to night's embrace,
Find your joy in this timeless grace.
For in the shadows and in the light,
Life's choreography is pure delight.

Resonant Silhouettes

Figures linger in the dimming light,
Memories etched, soft and bright.
In the fading twilight, shadows grow,
A gallery where feelings flow.

Ghosts of laughter in the eve's glow,
Each silence holds what we both know.
The world a stage for those we miss,
In phantom forms, we reminisce.

Frames of moments, carved in air,
Resonant silhouettes whisper care.
Entwined spirits in twilight's hue,
Sharing secrets that once rang true.

As stars emerge, the night unveils,
Stories hidden in moonlit trails.
Every contour and every line,
A testament to love, divine.

In the quiet, echoes remain,
Of laughter, joy, and bittersweet pain.
Embrace the shadows, let them tell,
Of the resonant tales we know well.

Unraveled Unity

Threads of color woven tight,
A tapestry in soft twilight.
Differences blend, their beauty fun,
In the dance of many, we become one.

Hearts entwined in a gentle fold,
Each story shared is a thread of gold.
Diverse paths in the hands of fate,
Creating harmony that won't abate.

Voices rise in a joyful hymn,
In unity, our lights will dim.
Through trials faced and battles fought,
Together, stronger, we are sought.

In every heartbeat, a shared embrace,
Cultures blend in a sacred space.
With open arms and minds so free,
In our differences, we find the key.

So let us celebrate and sing our song,
In the fabric of life, we all belong.
As colorful threads weave the grand design,
Unraveled unity, a hope divine.

The Gentle Unison of Evening

As shadows weave their soft embrace,
The sun dips low, a golden grace.
Whispers of night begin to blend,
In harmony, the day will end.

Crickets sing their lullabies,
Underneath the painted skies.
Stars peek out, a twinkling show,
Where dreams and starlight gently flow.

The breeze carries a sweet refrain,
A gentle touch, a soft, warm rain.
Leaves rustle in the cooling air,
A tranquil pause, a moment rare.

Colors fade to muted hue,
As twilight bathes the world anew.
In this hush, where silence thrives,
Life finds peace, and nature jives.

The moon casts silver beams so bright,
A guiding light through endless night.
In the gentle unison found,
All of life's beauty knows no bound.

Where Earth Meets the Celestial Tide

Beneath the sky, where oceans sigh,
The stars above begin to fly.
Waves clash softly on the shore,
An ancient dance, forevermore.

The horizon blurs with evening's glow,
As tides pull back, then gently flow.
In whispered secrets, the night unveils,
Stories told in the wind's sweet trails.

The moon ascends, a silver crown,
Casting dreams through the entire town.
In shadows deep, life takes its flight,
Where earth meets the celestial light.

Seashells whisper stories bold,
Of distant lands and treasures told.
Each wave a tale of love and loss,
In the vastness, no path is glossed.

Connect and drift within this tide,
In the serene space, let worries slide.
Where earth and sky together weave,
A tapestry that hearts believe.

Tranquil Reflections of the Evening Star

The evening star begins to shine,
In velvet skies, a light divine.
With every twinkle, a wish takes flight,
A moment captured, a dream ignites.

Rippling waters mirror the glow,
Calm reflections in a steady flow.
Whispers dance upon the lake,
A tranquil peace that hearts awake.

As shadows deepen with the night,
A soft embrace, a pure delight.
Nature's breath in harmony,
Cocooned here in serenity.

Petals close to rest their heads,
Underneath the starlit spreads.
Each breeze shifts time, a gentle flow,
Cradling dreams as night winds blow.

In this silence, all is clear,
With every heartbeat, dreams draw near.
Tranquil moments softly pass,
In starlit memories, we amass.

Chronicles of the Sunset's Embrace

Golden hues in the evening light,
Fade to shades of calm and quiet.
Horizons blaze with fearless fire,
As day retreats to night's desire.

Each sunset tells a tale profound,
Of journeys taken, lost and found.
The sky, a canvas rich and wide,
Paints memories where dreams abide.

With every shade, a story spins,
Of laughter shared and where love begins.
In every blush, a heart will sigh,
As time whispers its soft goodbye.

The earth breathes deep, a gentle pause,
In twilight's grasp, nature's cause.
Chronicles woven in the dusk,
Celebrate life in shades we trust.

As stars emerge to light the way,
We hold close the dusk's soft sway.
In the sunset's embrace, we find,
A treasure wrapped in peace of mind.

Lullabies of the Luminous

Stars whisper softly in the night,
Dreams take flight, hearts feel light.
Moonbeams dance on slumber's shore,
Cradled in shadows, we seek more.

Gentle breezes sing a tune,
Embracing magic beneath the moon.
Silver beams in twilight's glow,
Guide our thoughts where wishes flow.

Rest comes wrapped in velvet skies,
Where distant echoes softly rise.
Each note a promise, pure, divine,
In quiet twilight, our souls entwine.

As silence falls, the world retreats,
In this haven, solace meets.
Close your eyes and find your place,
In luminous dreams, a warm embrace.

With every sigh, the stars align,
Lullabies of light are thine.
In gentle rhythms, whispers weave,
In this night, we truly believe.

The Song of Still Waters

Reflecting light, the stillness gleams,
Echoes of nature, fluid dreams.
Ripples carry forgotten tales,
Where whispered winds weave silver trails.

Crisp air dances o'er the lake,
Carrying secrets it can't forsake.
Tranquil moments in quiet grace,
Each glance a glimpse, each breath a space.

Beneath the surface, life swells near,
In silence, all becomes so clear.
Time slows down, the world shall wait,
In still waters, we contemplate.

Together, we wander this serene shore,
Where echoes linger, and spirits soar.
Nature's calm, a soothing balm,
Reminding us of peace, of calm.

As shadows stretch, the day must yield,
While twilight opens the artist's field.
In the quiet, hearts entwine,
In this song, our dreams align.

Merging Realms of Wonder

In twilight's grasp where shadows blend,
Imagination flows, no end.
Starlit skies beckoning near,
Whispers of joy, free of fear.

Hearts ignite, bursts of delight,
As worlds converge, spirits take flight.
Colors merge in vibrant streams,
A tapestry woven from our dreams.

Glimmers of magic spark the night,
Awakening visions, pure and bright.
In this dance, no fear nor doubt,
Merging realms, we've figured it out.

Every heartbeat creates a thread,
Binding stories where all are led.
The universe sings, a cosmic sound,
In wonder's arms, we're forever bound.

So take my hand, let's journey wide,
Through paths of dreams, side by side.
Together we'll paint the endless skies,
In merging realms, our spirits rise.

A Canvas of Shared Dreams

On a canvas where colors blend,
Each stroke a whisper that will not end.
Heartbeats echo, souls collide,
In dreams we share, there's no divide.

Brushes dipped in hopes and fears,
Masterpieces crafted through the years.
Every hue a tale retold,
A thousand stories waiting bold.

Together we sketch the world anew,
Bound by visions, pure and true.
In gentle strokes, our spirits sing,
Painting joy in everything.

As twilight breaks, the colors flow,
A radiant path where dreamers go.
Every glance ignites a spark,
A canvas lit, lighting the dark.

With every stroke, we weave our fate,
In this masterpiece, we celebrate.
Hand in hand, we'll create and mend,
A canvas of dreams that never end.

Tides of Tranquility Unfolding

Soft waves whisper to the shore,
Embracing secrets evermore.
Moonlit paths on water's dance,
In this moment, hearts entrance.

Gentle breezes weave through grass,
Caressing leaves as shadows pass.
Nature's song in twilight sings,
In silence, peace the spirit brings.

Stars awaken, skies unfold,
Stories in their glimmers told.
Each heartbeat flows with silent grace,
Tides of calm in time and space.

Bridges of Light Across the Horizon

Colors bloom as daylight fades,
Painting paths where warmth invades.
Golden beams through clouds extend,
Building bridges that transcend.

Footsteps wander, dreams awake,
Harmony in every lake.
Reflections dance in twilight's glow,
As whispers of the night wind blow.

Together we can find the way,
Through the night into the day.
Every heartbeat, every sigh,
A bridge of light against the sky.

The Language of Light and Air

Sunbeams touch the waking trees,
Speaking softly through the breeze.
In every rustle, life confides,
A sacred truth that softly guides.

Clouds unravel, stories spun,
Words of silence, one by one.
The air weaves tales of far-off lands,
In nature's grasp, we understand.

Each glimmer, every sigh we share,
Whispers of the earth laid bare.
In the twilight's gentle embrace,
The language plays, pure and chaste.

When All is One in the Sky

Above us spreads a canvas wide,
Where dreams and stars in silence glide.
A universe of hopes unchained,
In unity, our hearts remained.

With every twinkle, wishes soar,
A bond connects forevermore.
The night enfolds us, warm and bright,
In this moment, all feels right.

When shadows blend and daylight wanes,
In twilight's glow, love remains.
Together, lost in endless sighs,
When all is one beneath the skies.

The Serenity Between Stars

In the quiet night, they glow,
Whispers of light, soft and slow.
Each star a dream, each twinkle a sigh,
In the vast canvas, we wonder why.

Cosmic whispers, secrets untold,
Stories of ages, mysteries bold.
Between the stars, a dance takes flight,
In harmony's embrace, lost in the night.

Galaxies spin in silence deep,
While celestial keepers watch and weep.
Each moment a spark, fleeting and bright,
A promise of peace in the dark's delight.

Serenity reigns, far from the noise,
In the black expanse, infinite joys.
Wrapped in the velvet of night's gentle hand,
We find our solace, we learn to understand.

Here in the stillness, we breathe as one,
Lost in the beauty, until the dawn.
In the calmness of space, our fears reside,
In the serenity found, we abide.

Rhythms of the Awakening

Soft hues blush as dawn creeps near,
Nature awakens, vibrant and clear.
Birds herald the sun with joyful calls,
In this symphony, the stillness falls.

Gentle breezes weave through the trees,
Dancing leaves whisper their secrets with ease.
Each note a promise, each sound a rhyme,
Guiding the world to the pulse of time.

Mountains rise, kissed by light,
Echoes of shadows retreating from sight.
Streams glisten bright, laughter in flow,
In this emerging dance, we grow.

Each heartbeat resonates, alive and true,
In the golden hue, we find what's due.
With every breath, the world comes awake,
In this rhythm of life, we choose to partake.

Together we rise as shadows depart,
Embracing the warmth that ignites the heart.
In the symphony of nature, we find our song,
And with it, the hope to which we belong.

Echoes of Unity in Dusk

As the sun bows down, colors entwine,
A tapestry woven with threads divine.
The day exhales, whispers of peace,
In the dusk's embrace, all worries cease.

Softly, the stars begin to gleam,
Each one a beacon, a distant dream.
With every heartbeat, the night draws near,
In the twilight glow, we hold what's dear.

Crickets sing, a chorus of night,
In their serenade, we find our light.
Moments shared, hearts beat as one,
In the whispers of dusk, we have begun.

Moonlight weaves through the silent trees,
Kissing the earth with a gentle breeze.
In this stillness, we intertwine,
Bound by the echoes, by design.

Together we stand in harmony's glow,
In unity's arms, we learn and grow.
As dusk settles softly, we find our way,
In the sacred silence, love will stay.

Whispers of the Distant Sky

Above the world, a canvas wide,
Stars speak softly, where secrets hide.
In the distance, dreams weave and play,
Guiding our hearts, leading the way.

Clouds drift gently, like thoughts in flight,
Carrying whispers of day and night.
The horizon blushes, kissed by the sun,
In the tapestry of time, we are one.

Galaxies shimmer, histories unfold,
Stories of past that never grow old.
In this vastness, we long to explore,
Finding our place, forevermore.

Twinkling lights offer hope from afar,
A glimpse of the magic in every star.
In the serene silence, we hear their call,
Echoes of wisdom, inviting us all.

So let us listen to the skies above,
For in their whispers, we find our love.
In the embrace of the night, we shall soar,
In the symphony of stars, forevermore.

Ballet of the Elements Unleashed

Wind brushes softly on the cheek,
Leaves dance lightly, a song unique.
Water twirls, reflecting light,
In this ballet of day and night.

Fire flickers, a vibrant blaze,
Heat and color set the stage.
Earth holds steady, grounded tight,
While stars begin their twinkling flight.

Lightning splits the darkened sky,
Thunder echoes, a booming cry.
Each element in graceful stride,
Together they perform with pride.

Harmony in every clash,
Nature's rhythm, a sudden flash.
As mountains rise and rivers flow,
The dance continues, hearts aglow.

All unite, both fierce and free,
In this vast, wild symphony.
The elements weave a tale profound,
In their ballet, magic is found.

Weaving Whispers Through the Twilight

In twilight's embrace, shadows stretch long,
Whispers of dusk, a delicate song.
Stars peek through the deepening veil,
Night's gentle breath begins to sail.

The crescent moon, a silver smile,
Guides lost dreams for a little while.
Soft winds carry stories untold,
In this hour, mysteries unfold.

Fireflies twinkle, tiny beacons bright,
Chasing the remnants of fading light.
Each step we take, a fleeting chance,
In the dusk, the world seems to dance.

The horizon fades, colors blend,
Time slows down, as moments suspend.
In twilight's glow, we find our way,
Embracing the magic that calls to stay.

A tapestry woven with stars and sighs,
In the quiet, our hopes arise.
Whispers linger, soft as a sigh,
Through twilight's calm, we learn to fly.

Canvas of the Infinite Unfolding

Brushstrokes of dreams on a canvas vast,
Colors collide, present meets past.
Each hue a whisper, each line a thought,
In this art, all battles are fought.

The palette dances, alive with grace,
Shapes emerge, take form in space.
A heartbeat pulses through the paint,
Each work a message, our souls acquaint.

Infinite tales in each stroke reside,
Textures of laughter, of tearful pride.
In chaos and order, beauty reflects,
Life's essence captured; love intersects.

Layers build up, stories entwined,
With every stroke, new worlds are defined.
The canvas breathes, alive, awake,
An endless journey we choose to take.

As the final hues begin to blend,
The masterpiece whispers, "This is not the end."
For in every blank space, hopes yet to find,
A canvas unfurls, forever unlined.

The Quiet Symphony of the Field

In the field where wildflowers sway,
Nature hums its gentle ballet.
Grass whispers secrets to the breeze,
While clouds drift slowly, as they please.

Morning dew glistens like tiny pearls,
In sunlight's warmth, the magic unfurls.
A chorus of crickets serenade night,
With fireflies joining, a flickering light.

Each heartbeat echoes through the land,
Together they form a timeless band.
Birds take flight, singing their song,
In the quiet symphony, we all belong.

The rustle of leaves, a calming sound,
In nature's embrace, peace is found.
As time wanders on, with every breath,
The field tells stories of life and death.

Embrace the stillness, let worries cease,
In the quiet, we discover peace.
Every note, a reminder to feel,
For life is a symphony, ever real.

Threads of Color in the Evening's Hand

The sun dips low, a fiery hue,
Pinks and golds in skies of blue.
Each stroke a memory, softly spun,
As day surrenders to night's fun.

Gentle breezes whisper near,
Brushing softly, sweet and clear.
Canvas wide, the dusk unfurls,
Painting dreams in twilight swirls.

Clouds drift by, like thoughts untold,
Wrapped in hues—both warm and cold.
Each shade a story, bright yet faint,
In this show, the world's a saint.

Stars peer out, the night is young,
A tapestry of songs unsung.
Fading light, yet hearts remain,
In vibrant whispers, joy and pain.

So gather close, see colors blend,
In every shade, find a friend.
Here in twilight, magic flows,
In threads of color, beauty grows.

Celestial Convergence in the Starlight

Two souls align beneath the sky,
Where cosmic wonders softly lie.
Galaxies glance in radiant dance,
Eternity wraps them in a trance.

Whispers of stars echo above,
Cascading like a timeless love.
Nebulas bloom in hues so rare,
A celestial embrace, beyond compare.

Planets spin in the vast unknown,
While fate pulls strings, gently sewn.
Hearts beat fast, a cosmic call,
In starlit shadows, we find it all.

Moments captured in fleeting light,
Guiding our path through the night.
With every spark, a promise made,
In the universe, dreams never fade.

So let us dance under the moon,
Find solace in this ancient tune.
In the stillness, let us unite,
In celestial convergence, hold on tight.

The Romance of Light and Shadow

In twilight's glow, they intertwine,
Light and shadow, a dance divine.
With soft caresses, they embrace,
Creating magic in every space.

The sun's warm kiss, a golden frame,
While shadows whisper, calling names.
Together they weave a tale so deep,
In their romance, secrets keep.

Flickering flames on the wall's embrace,
Shifting forms that time can't trace.
With every flicker, a heartbeat sings,
A longing formed as night time clings.

Reflection's glow, a fleeting dance,
They nurture hope in a daring glance.
Moments gleaned in stark contrast,
Find beauty in what's meant to last.

So let their love illuminate our days,
In gentle hues, in myriad ways.
For every shadow holds a light,
In the romance of day and night.

Tracing the Echoes of Nature's Heart

In whispered woods where secrets tread,
Nature's language softly spread.
Leaves flutter down like notes divine,
Tracing echoes where stars align.

Mountains stand, ancient and bold,
Holding stories that time has told.
Rivers sing with gentle flow,
In every curve, their heartbeats show.

The rustling grass, a quiet sigh,
As breezes dance, and spirits fly.
Wildflowers bloom, in colors bright,
Painting meadows with sheer delight.

With every dawn, the earth awakes,
In harmony, the world remakes.
Sculpting wonders in dusk's embrace,
In nature's heart, we find our place.

So step outside, breathe deep the air,
Feel the pulse of life laid bare.
In nature's song, find peace and art,
Tracing echoes of its heart.

Ascent to Tranquil Realms

The path winds softly through the trees,
Each step a whisper, carried by the breeze.
In shadows where the stillness sings,
The heart finds peace in simple things.

Above, the sky begins to clear,
As sunlight warms the morning near.
The burdens of the past release,
In this bright moment, I find my peace.

With every breath, a gentle climb,
The soul ascends beyond all time.
Here in this realm, all worries cease,
And in the silence, I find my ease.

The mountaintops hold tales untold,
In nature's arms, I feel so bold.
The world below fades far from view,
A tranquil heart finds strength anew.

As day meets night, the stars ignite,
Guiding the way with soft, pure light.
In this ascent, my spirit soars,
To tranquil realms where love restores.

When Colors Embrace the Dawn

A canvas stretched across the sky,
Brushstrokes of pink where dreams can fly.
The dawn awakens in soft hues,
Painting a world with vibrant views.

The gold spills brightly on the sea,
Mirroring hope, wild and free.
As shadows fade, the whispers grow,
In morning's glow, my spirit flows.

Each ray of light a tender kiss,
Awakening all in pure bliss.
The flowers dance to nature's tune,
As colors mingle with the moon.

The chirping songs of morning's choir,
Lift the heart, inspire the fire.
In sacred moments, life unfolds,
With every brush of bright and bold.

As dawn breaks bright, the world aligns,
In unity where love entwines.
When colors meet and dreams take flight,
The dawn ignites the dark of night.

Serenade of the Setting Sun

The sun dips low, a fiery blaze,
A serenade in golden rays.
With every note, the day concedes,
As twilight whispers through the trees.

Brush strokes of crimson in the sky,
While softening clouds drift gently by.
The horizon blurs at day's sweet end,
As evening graces us to mend.

Below, the world begins to sigh,
As stars awaken in the sky.
A lullaby from earth to sky,
Where dreams are born, and hopes can fly.

In this embrace, I find my peace,
A tranquil heart that will not cease.
Each moment savored, time stands still,
As evening dances, night will thrill.

With every hue, a story spun,
In harmony, the night has won.
The serenade of the setting sun,
A melody, united as one.

Chords of Celestial Echoes

In silence deep, the cosmos hums,
With chords of echoes, softly strums.
The stars align in radiant play,
Whispering secrets of the day.

Galaxies twirl in dreamy flight,
A symphony beneath the light.
Each note a spark, a wish afloat,
In this vast sea, our hearts do boat.

The moon cradles the night so still,
Crafting shadows with gentle thrill.
Through the darkness, the voices rise,
In celestial dances, we touch the skies.

Hear the music in the breeze,
Nature's heart amidst the trees.
Every leaf plays a tune so sweet,
As harmony and earth do meet.

With every breath, the universe sings,
In chords of magic, love's own wings.
In echoes bright, our spirits soar,
Finding the peace we've sought before.

Embracing the Sky's Sweet Solitude

Beneath the vast and quiet blue,
A whisper lingers, soft and true.
Clouds dance gently in the air,
An embrace of peace, beyond compare.

Waves of stillness brush my skin,
As daylight fades, the stars begin.
In twilight's glow, I find my way,
To cherish moments, come what may.

The silence sings, a tender song,
In solitude, I feel I belong.
Each breath a gift, a time to pause,
Embracing life without a cause.

Above the trees, the shadows play,
Nature whispers, guiding my stay.
In the warmth of dusk, I find my rest,
The quiet heart knows what is best.

As night descends, the world transforms,
In calming darkness, my spirit warms.
Underneath the sky's embrace,
I find my peace in this sacred space.

Narratives of Color and Light

Morning bursts in hues so bright,
The canvas wakes, alive with light.
Each petal glows in golden gleam,
A chorus sings, a vibrant dream.

Shadows dance on the ancient stone,
Every hue tells stories known.
Laughter echoes in the breeze,
Art unfolds beneath the trees.

Crimson skies at dusk ignite,
A tale of day, embracing night.
Soft whispers in the garden bloom,
Colors blend and chase the gloom.

Reflections shimmer on the stream,
Watching nature weave its dream.
Each tone a voice, each shade a clue,
Life's grand tapestry comes into view.

As stars awaken, silver and cool,
The night paints shades, the heart's true jewel.
In every moment, colors sing,
Life's vibrant stories, ever spring.

Dreams Adrift in Celestial Spaces

In quiet night, the dreams take flight,
On velvet wings, they roam the night.
Stars are lanterns, guiding true,
In celestial spaces, old and new.

A tapestry of wishes spun,
Beneath the moon, the heart will run.
Floating softly, a gentle sigh,
With hopes that reach the endless sky.

Galaxies whisper, secrets shared,
In cosmic realms, no soul is scared.
Each dream a spark, a distant light,
Adrift in wonder, lost from sight.

Nebulas swirl, colors collide,
In this vastness, I must confide.
Every thought a shooting star,
Carving paths from near to far.

Embracing night, I claim my flight,
To dance among the stars so bright.
In dreams adrift, I find my peace,
Within the universe, my heart's release.

Requiem for Distant Stars

Once they shone, a guiding light,
In the canvas dark, a song in flight.
Faded whispers mark their grave,
As echoes call from the cosmic wave.

Tales of fire in the velvet sky,
Now they flicker, a muted sigh.
Lost in the void's eternal song,
A requiem for the brave and strong.

Ghostly trails of light and dust,
In silence, we place our trust.
Each twinkle fades, a story told,
In the embrace of the night so cold.

Yet in the dark, a spark remains,
A memory where beauty reigns.
For every heart that yearns and sighs,
The distant stars live on in eyes.

In stardust dreams, they still reside,
In memory's light, they've never died.
Their legacy in the twilight gleams,
A requiem for eternal dreams.

Celestial Echoes

Stars shimmer in the night sky,
Whispers of dreams drift high,
The moon beams a silver light,
   Guiding lost souls in flight.

Galaxies spin in rhythm,
A cosmic dance, a hymn,
Shooting stars trail their grace,
   In the vast, endless space.

Waves of light cascade down,
Painting skies of velvet brown,
The universe sings its song,
Binding all where we belong.

Time slips through starlit hands,
In vast and silent lands,
Echoes of the past return,
Lighting up our hearts that burn.

Heavenly bodies embrace,
In the dark, they find their place,
A symphony on full display,
   Celestial echoes guide our way.

Whispered Melodies

Soft rains fall on tender leaves,
Nature's breath so gently weaves,
Every rustle, every sigh,
A melody floating by.

Birds call out with morning light,
Their songs resound, a pure delight,
In the stillness, secrets blend,
Whispered tunes that never end.

The breeze carries tales untold,
Of love and life, both brave and bold,
Through the trees, their voices soar,
Lifting hearts forevermore.

In twilight's hush, a lullaby,
Stars awaken in the sky,
Every twinkle, every gleam,
Plays the notes of nature's dream.

Harmony in twilight's hue,
Melodies of old and new,
With each echo, spirits rise,
Whispered songs beneath the skies.

Tides of Tranquility

Gentle waves kiss the shore,
A soothing rhythm we adore,
Seashells whisper tales of yore,
In endless cycles, evermore.

Moonlit paths lead us home,
Beneath the stars, we freely roam,
In tranquil moments, hearts entwined,
In nature's arms, peace we find.

Rippling waters, calm and deep,
Cradle dreams in peaceful sleep,
Every wave a silent prayer,
Binding souls in tender care.

Sunrise paints the ocean's face,
A golden glow, a warm embrace,
With every tide, a chance to breathe,
In nature's grace, we believe.

Soft horizons stretch afar,
Guiding hearts like a distant star,
In waves of calm, we drift along,
Tides of tranquility, our song.

Symphony of Sunsets

Crimson hues kiss the fading light,
Day surrenders to the night,
Beneath the canvas of the sky,
Whispers of goodbyes float by.

Clouds painted in golden seams,
Dancing lightly in our dreams,
With each brushstroke, time takes flight,
As shadows blend with fading light.

The horizon sings a final tune,
A fleeting glimpse of the silver moon,
Nature's chorus, soft and sweet,
In this moment, our hearts meet.

As the stars awaken one by one,
The day departs, the night's begun,
Every whisper in the air,
Carries stories softly shared.

With every sunset, souls connect,
In vibrant colors, we reflect,
Life's grand symphony unfolds,
In sunsets painted, dreams consoled.

Celestial Mosaic of Unity

Stars whisper secrets in the night,
Each twinkle a tale of shared light.
Galaxies dance in cosmic embrace,
A tapestry woven in time and space.

Together we rise, hearts intertwined,
Echoes of laughter in moonlight combined.
Boundless horizons, our dreams take flight,
In the celestial weave, we shine ever bright.

Fragments of stardust, lost yet found,
In every heartbeat, the universe sounds.
Harmony sings in the vastness wide,
A mosaic of unity, forever our guide.

From deep within the silence, we soar,
In the gentle hush, we crave for more.
Connected as one, through the grand design,
In this celestial mosaic, our spirits align.

Floating through galaxies, hand in hand,
We leave our footprints in stardust sand.
In the embrace of night, collide and blend,
A celestial chorus that never will end.

The Elixir of Twilight's Joy

The sun dips low, a fiery glow,
Day's last whisper setting hearts aglow.
Shadows stretch and the night draws near,
In twilight's embrace, joy crystallizes clear.

A symphony of colors paints the sky,
With each fading hue, hopes learn to fly.
Breezes carry laughter, light and free,
In the elixir of dusk, we find harmony.

Stars awaken in soft, gentle grace,
Each one a promise, a secret place.
Under the serenade of twilight's charm,
We lose our worries, wrapped in its calm.

Moments dissolve in the lavender light,
Every heartbeat syncs with the quiet night.
In this fleeting magic, we taste our dreams,
The elixir of joy flows in blissful streams.

Together we dance on the edge of night,
Guided by whispers of fading sunlight.
Every spark ignites our souls to play,
In the twilight's embrace, we'll forever stay.

Rhapsody of the Infinite Sky

Above our heads, a symphony swells,
In the vast expanse where wonder dwells.
Clouds drift like notes in a melodic dance,
An infinite canvas where spirits prance.

Each dawn heralds a fresh serenade,
As colors awaken, dreams are laid.
Winds carry whispers of distant place,
In the rhapsody sung by the sky's grace.

Stars punctuate the evening's refrain,
With sparkling gems in a velvet domain.
In celestial concert, our souls expand,
Embracing the night, hand in hand.

From horizon's edge to celestial sea,
We lose ourselves in the boundless spree.
In the echo of night, we find our way,
In the rhapsody of the infinite play.

With breaths of wonder and hearts aglow,
We weave our tales where the starlight flows.
Together we marvel at life's grand design,
In the embrace of the sky, our spirits entwine.

Serenity Found Between the Lines

In the quiet corners of whispered thoughts,
Where silence lingers, and time begot.
Words flow softly like currents of air,
A stillness blooms, delicate and rare.

Pages unfold with stories untold,
Ink stains the fabric of dreams made bold.
Between the lines, a universe glows,
Serenity sprouts where the heart knows.

Breathe in the pauses, the spaces between,
In moments of silence, the truth is gleaned.
Thoughts entwine gently, like vines in spring,
In the garden of prose, endless blooms bring.

Each line a heartbeat, a pulse, a sigh,
In the rhythm of life, we question why.
Yet within those pauses, compassion shines,
As serenity whispers from between the lines.

Together we weave tales of the mind,
In the ever-flowing, the truth we find.
In the gentle margins where dreams collide,
Serenity awaits, ever our guide.

The Dance of Distant Peaks

In shadows cast by mountain crowns,
The winds do weave their whispered sounds.
Each peak stands proud, a silent sage,
With stories locked in time's own cage.

Beneath a sky of azure blue,
The valleys hold the morning dew.
A dance of light, the sun does play,
On rugged heights, both bold and gay.

Clouds drift by in gentle streams,
They carry forth our wildest dreams.
The echoes of the past unite,
In harmony with day and night.

With every step, the heart will soar,
To peaks that promise evermore.
In nature's arms, we find our peace,
Where all our worries find release.

So come and tread on sacred ground,
Where silent heights with love abound.
In distant peaks, our souls will find,
The dance of life that's intertwined.

Threads of Serene Skies

Beneath the pall of twilight's grace,
The stars adorn the vast embrace.
A tapestry of light unfolds,
In secrets spun, the night beholds.

The moonlight bathes us, soft and pale,
As whispers weave a tender tale.
Each thread a dream, each wish a sigh,
That floats amidst the velvet sky.

With every heartbeat, time takes flight,
In the gentle folds of endless night.
The cosmos dances, bright and free,
A symphony of unity.

In this embrace, we find our place,
Amongst the stars, a warm embrace.
The tranquil pulse of space and time,
In every breath, a quiet rhyme.

So dive into the starlit sea,
And let your spirit wander free.
For in each thread, a story's spun,
Beneath the vast, eternal sun.

Kaleidoscope of Whispered Dreams

In twilight glow, the colors blend,
A canvas where the heart can mend.
With every hue, a secret shared,
In whispered dreams, we are prepared.

The laughter lifts on gentle breeze,
As petals dance from blossomed trees.
In vibrant shades, our spirits soar,
To chase the waves on distant shore.

A kaleidoscope of sights and sounds,
Where every joy and sorrow bounds.
The echoes of our hopes arise,
In playful forms that mesmerize.

With open hearts, we find our way,
Through winding paths of night and day.
In every twist, a lesson learned,
In every turn, a passion burned.

So let us dance on dreams unspun,
To weave a tale as bright as sun.
In colors bold, we find our theme,
A world alive with whispered dreams.

A Harmony Born from Dusk

As day departs, the shadows creep,
A hush descends, the world's asleep.
In twilight's arms, the calm resides,
Where whispers merge with ebbing tides.

The horizon glows with embered light,
A promise born of fading night.
In every heartbeat, silence hums,
As nightingale's soft music strums.

The stars awaken, one by one,
Their twinkling charm, a gentle fun.
In darkness deep, we find our way,
A melody that bids us stay.

With every breath, the night unfolds,
Its mysteries in shadows told.
In harmony, our spirits blend,
Where dusk and dreams begin to mend.

So let us embrace this dusky grace,
As time moves on at its own pace.
For in the night, our hearts will sing,
A harmony, a cherished thing.

The Touch of Dawn on a Still Heart

Morning whispers soft and low,
A gentle light begins to grow.
The cool breeze stirs the tranquil air,
As night dissolves in pale despair.

Promises of day arise,
Painting gold across the skies.
Each shadow fades, as hope ignites,
In the warmth of dawn's delights.

With every heartbeat, time renews,
Breathing life in vibrant hues.
Awakening dreams once held tight,
In the arms of soft twilight.

Waking stillness starts to hum,
Nature's chorus now begun.
The world stirs from its slumber deep,
While the heart begins to leap.

In the dawn's embrace, we sigh,
As day unfolds its endless sky.
Each moment blooms, a sacred part,
Forever touched, the still heart.

Caress of the Celestial Breeze

Whispers dance on evening's breath,
Carrying secrets of life and death.
Stars awaken, shimmering bright,
Guiding souls through the night.

Clouds drift softly, like a dream,
In the dark, they flicker and gleam.
A gentle touch upon the soul,
As night unfolds its silver scroll.

The breeze sweeps past, a lover's sigh,
Anticipation in the sky.
Every sigh a wish untold,
A promise of warmth when nights grow cold.

Through shadows thick, the night prevails,
Yet in darkness, love unveils.
A caress that stirs the heart,
Binding souls, never to part.

Beneath the stars, we're intertwined,
Past the worries, future aligned.
Where the celestial whispers weave,
A tapestry of dreams we believe.

Harmonies of the Fading Light

As daylight wanes, the colors blend,
Soft melodies of dusk ascend.
Crimson hues and whispers gray,
Guide the sun to end its day.

A tranquil hush fills the air,
Notes of stillness everywhere.
Reflecting on what once was bright,
Nature sings the fading light.

In the twilight's embrace, hearts soar,
A symphony that asks for more.
Each fleeting note, a sweet refrain,
Alive in moments, loss, and gain.

Even as shadows stretch and creep,
In their depths, our dreams do leap.
For every end brings forth a start,
In the harmonies of the heart.

Let the darkness hold your hand,
Feel the music, soft and grand.
As the light gently takes its flight,
We find solace in the night.

Reflections on the Kaleidoscope Sky

Oh, the colors twist and twirl,
A universe in perfect swirl.
Each moment shifts, a vivid sight,
Crafting dreams in pure delight.

Clouds mingle in playful dance,
Life awakens in every chance.
Mirroring hope in every hue,
The sky sings soft, inviting you.

Catch the fragments drifting by,
Fragments of the kaleidoscope sky.
Each memory a vibrant shard,
Painting life, both bold and scarred.

In the twilight's embrace, we gaze,
Lost in wonder, softly amazed.
As day yields to night's embrace,
We find our dreams in time and space.

Let the spectrum guide your soul,
With every shift, find your goal.
In a world of break and mend,
Let the night beneath stars extend.

The Soft Song of the Universe Making Peace

In the quiet night, stars begin to hum,
A melody of worlds, where dreams can come.
Whispers of the cosmos, gentle and clear,
Bringing hearts together, casting out fear.

Galaxies dance in a shimmering waltz,
Revealing the magic, in rhythms that halt.
Celestial echoes weave stories untold,
Of love in the cosmos, a tapestry bold.

The moon cradles secrets in silver embrace,
As soft winds carry peace through infinite space.
Harmony lingers, a soothing refrain,
In the soft song of stars, we find no pain.

Unbound by the distance, our spirits unite,
In the warmth of the universe, darkness turns light.
Each note a reminder, we're never alone,
In this vast symphony, we've all found a home.

The Reflection of Light Within Us

In the depths of the heart, a spark softly glows,
Illuminating pathways where true beauty flows.
Mirrors of kindness reflect in our eyes,
Showing the world our compassionate ties.

Shadows may linger, yet light shall remain,
A beacon of hope in moments of pain.
Each soul a canvas, painted by fate,
With colors of love, we intricately create.

Through valleys of doubt, we rise and we shine,
Unfolding the treasures, the stars that align.
The journey is sacred, every step we take,
Reveals the reflection, for unity's sake.

In whispers of dusk, our spirits will soar,
Awakening magic, revealing the core.
For within every being, a light can ignite,
Together we flourish, in the warmth of our light.

Verses From the Edge of Infinity

On the cusp of the void, where time loses track,
Thoughts spin like comets, never looking back.
Each moment a brushstroke, on eternity's canvas,
As we write our own fate with dreams that can manage.

Galaxies whisper tales of ancient lore,
Echoes of existence forever explore.
Through portals of wonder, we dance with delight,
Collecting the wisdom from the edge of night.

Journeying onward, through dark and through light,
Discovering realms that shimmer and excite.
With every new heartbeat, the universe grows,
In the spaces between, a garden that flows.

Beyond the horizon, mysteries abound,
Where silence and beauty are truly profound.
Our verses unveil what the stars want to share,
A declaration of life, with love in the air.

Chronicles of a Celestial Journey

In the tapestry of stars, our journey begins,
A voyage through cosmos, where infinite spins.
Every heartbeat a compass, every breath a song,
Guiding us forward, where we all belong.

We sail on the winds of a cosmic embrace,
Charting the heavens, exploring their grace.
With each new horizon, adventures unfold,
In chronicles written in stardust and gold.

The whispers of comets, the tales of the night,
Remind us of magic, of love's pure light.
Through nebulae swirling, through voids ever vast,
We find our reflection, present and past.

In moments of silence, we dwell in the awe,
Embracing the wonders, those unspoken laws.
Together we wander, our spirits take flight,
In chronicles carved from the depths of the night.

Overture of Nature's Embrace

In lush green fields where wildflowers play,
The whispers of wind carry laughter at bay.
Beneath the wide sky, the clouds gently drift,
Nature's soft embrace is the world's greatest gift.

Mountains stand tall, their peaks kissed by light,
A symphony of colors ignites the night.
Rivers sing songs in a melodious flow,
In each corner of earth, the beauty will grow.

The sun bids adieu as it sinks in the west,
An artist at work, creating a jest.
Owls call for peace, while the stars take their flight,
A canvas of dreams born from day into night.

In quiet of woods, where shadows entwine,
The moon blankets all with a silvery line.
Crickets are crooning their twilight refrain,
While nature unfolds her sweet, sacred chain.

Every heartbeat echoes in harmony's song,
Nature's embrace weaves us together so strong.
In each fleeting moment, we find our own space,
The world whispers softly, in nature's embrace.

Beyond the Veil of Dusk and Dawn

When twilight descends and shadows grow long,
A tapestry weaves, where spirits belong.
The horizon glimmers with hues amber bright,
Beyond the veil whispers a comforting light.

As stars awaken in an indigo sea,
The universe sings to the heart wild and free.
Each twinkle a tale from the distant past,
A reminder that moments are meant to last.

The days ebb away, like waves on the shore,
Grains of our memories, we gather and store.
With every dawn breaking, new hopes will arise,
A canvas of dreams painted across the skies.

Beyond the horizon, where the sun starts its flight,
A promise of brilliance, a symphony bright.
We chase after shadows, yet live in the now,
In every heartbeat, we honor the vow.

In this dance of transitions, we're gently entwined,
A cycle eternal, through life we will find.
So here by the twilight, we quietly pause,
To cherish the moments, and nature's applause.

Echoing Dreams of the Open Air

Beneath the vast sky, we wander and roam,
Each breath a reminder of nature's sweet home.
The rustling leaves share secrets with me,
As whispers of wind brush through every tree.

Mountains call softly, their peaks full of grace,
Inviting the weary to find their own place.
With each step we take on the soft, verdant sod,
We're one with the earth, at peace with our God.

The sun's golden rays awaken the day,
Chasing away shadows, lighting the way.
In fields of wildflowers, dreams take their flight,
Each petal a promise, a spark in the light.

Clouds wave goodbye as they drift on the breeze,
Time dances with echoes, flirting with trees.
In the bounty of nature, our souls take their share,
Resounding with joy in the open air.

So let's chase horizons, let's sing to the sky,
Together we'll laugh, and together we'll cry.
In echoing dreams where our spirits run free,
The open air beckons, inviting you and me.

Synthesis of Light and Life

In dawn's tender glow, the world comes alive,
With each ray of sunlight, the heart starts to thrive.
Nature awakens in a radiant trance,
A synthesis glorious, a cosmic dance.

The flowers unfurl, their colors ablaze,
Each petal a whisper, a moment to praise.
Birdsong fills the air, a melodic sweet sound,
In harmony's grasp, life circles around.

Rippling rivers echo with laughter and cheer,
Reflecting the beauty that gathers so near.
As trees stretch their arms to embrace the warm night,
A synthesis forming, both gentle and bright.

With twilight's embrace, the stars gently wink,
Inviting our dreams to drift, dance, and think.
In the quiet of night, beneath heavens wide,
We find our own selves, in the light we confide.

So let us celebrate this sacred design,
Where light meets with life, and our hearts intertwine.
Through seasons and cycles, may we remain kind,
In the synthesis vibrant, together we bind.

A Tapestry Woven in Clouds

Fluffy whispers drift on high,
Casting shadows in the sky.
Dreams entwined, a canvas fair,
Nature's brush paints everywhere.

Silver linings, golden rays,
Dancing light in soft ballet.
Winds carry tales of distant lands,
While time sifts through gentle hands.

Misty veils in twilight glow,
Echo whispers from below.
A quilt of wonders woven bright,
Cradles all in soft moonlight.

Through the currents, stories flow,
In each thread, a secret's glow.
Endless dreams spread out so wide,
On nature's canvas, we confide.

The Palette of a Peaceful Evening

Brushstrokes in a dusky hue,
Calming colors, shades anew.
Crimson, gold, and violet blend,
Whispers of the day's sweet end.

Birds retreat to nests of grace,
Nighttime wraps the earth in lace.
Stars peek out, like diamonds rare,
Telling tales in evening air.

Fields embrace the twilight's kiss,
Softly yielding, moments bliss.
As twilight gathers, shadows play,
Crickets serenade the day.

Gentle breezes softly sigh,
Brushing 'gainst the azure sky.
Nature draws a soothing breath,
In this pause, we find our rest.

Flights of Fancy Upon Warm Winds

Kites of laughter soar above,
Carried by the winds of love.
In the sky, our dreams take flight,
Dancing with the fading light.

Clouds like boats drift far and wide,
On the currents, hope does ride.
Weave the tales of all we seek,
In the whispers, strong yet meek.

Glimmers of tomorrow's dawn,
Painted where the dreams are drawn.
Every sigh, a story spun,
In the warmth of summer's sun.

Moments held by silky air,
Magic written everywhere.
Let your spirit freely roam,
In the blue, we find our home.

Songs of the Earth and Sky

Harmonies of stars and trees,
Nature hums with every breeze.
Melodies from rivers flow,
Whispered secrets, soft and low.

Mountains stand with voices grand,
Echoes of a sacred land.
Fields alive with joy and peace,
Where the heart will never cease.

Underneath the silver moon,
Nightingale sings a tender tune.
Rustling leaves, a symphony,
In the dark, we find the key.

From the soil, the flowers rise,
Painting stories in the skies.
All around, the rhythms blend,
Songs of life that never end.

The Dance of Light and Shadow

In quiet corners, shadows play,
They twist and turn, in soft ballet.
Light flickers bright, a gentle guide,
In the twilight's arms, they both reside.

Each moment breathes, a fleeting glance,
A whispered secret, a beckoning chance.
Together they weave, a tale untold,
In the fading warmth, as night turns cold.

The sun dips low, the colors blend,
A fusion found where curves extend.
Echoes of day in the moon's soft glow,
In the dance they share, an ebb and flow.

With every step, they shift and sway,
A waltz of dreams at the close of day.
Soft shadows linger, light slips away,
In their tender embrace, forever they'll stay.

As stars awaken in velvet skies,
A promise whispered without goodbyes.
For in the darkness, light finds its way,
In the dance of night and break of day.

Celestial Ballet of Dawn's Light

A soft blush rises, the world holds its breath,
As dawn spills colors, a gentle caress.
Whispers of morning, a choreographed flight,
Nature awakens in the warm golden light.

The birds take to air, a harmonious tune,
Their melodies echo beneath the pale moon.
With each rustle, leaves join the song,
In concert they dance, where all creatures belong.

The sun peeks shyly, a radiant sphere,
It chases away shadows, replacing with cheer.
A symphony blossoms, the earth's bright embrace,
In the heart of the moment, a sacred place.

Beams of fresh hope wash over the land,
Every blade of grass sparkles, so grand.
The sky stretches wide, in hues of soft pink,
In this timeless dance, all spirits link.

So let the dawn rise, with grace and delight,
In this celestial ballet of dawn's light.
Together we weave threads of the day,
In the beauty of morning, we find our way.

Echoes of a Golden Promise

Golden rays linger on the edge of night,
Softly they whisper, a promise in sight.
Through fields of dreams, emotions take flight,
In the echoes of joy, where hope burns bright.

The sun dips low, the horizon ablaze,
With memories crafted in warm, tender ways.
Whispers of laughter drift on the breeze,
In the heart of the moment, we find our ease.

Time stands still, wrapped in a glow,
Where dreams intertwine, and love begins to flow.
With every heartbeat, the promise is made,
In the softness of dusk, true colors invade.

Together we stand, hand in hand, so bold,
Facing the future, our story unfolds.
As twilight beckons, we cherish the past,
In echoes of love, we'll forever last.

The stars align, guiding our way,
In the pulse of the night, our spirits sway.
For every promise whispered beneath the sky,
Carries the echoes of dreams flying high.

In the Embrace of a New Day

Awaken, dear heart, the day softly calls,
With colors that shimmer on wide sunlit walls.
A fresh breeze dances, kisses the earth,
In the embrace of the day, find your rebirth.

The morning unfolds, a canvas so bright,
With strokes of nature, a breathtaking sight.
A chorus of life in the stillness, sings loud,
As you step forward, be brave and be proud.

With each step you take, new chances arise,
In the gentle warmth of the welcoming skies.
In laughter and love, your spirit ignites,
As shadows of doubt fade from your sights.

The sun stretches wide, its rays intertwine,
Embracing the world with warmth so divine.
In every heartbeat, cherish the play,
In the embrace of a new day, come what may.

As clouds drift above, painting stories anew,
Remember, dear soul, the journey is true.
With each moment cherished, let your heart sway,
In the embrace of a new day, forever stay.

Silent Chords of the Earth

In the hush of dawn's light,
Soft whispers fill the air,
Nature's song, oh so bright,
A harmony, pure and rare.

Mountains hold secrets deep,
Rivers flow with grace untold,
In silence, roots do creep,
Their stories, centuries old.

Leaves dance in the still breeze,
Branches sway with gentle ease,
Every sound, a subtle tease,
Nature's tune, a sweet reprise.

Footsteps light on winding trails,
Echoes of the world we tread,
Each heartbeat softly sails,
In the green, where dreams are fed.

Underneath the vast blue skies,
The earth whispers, waits, and sighs.

Embracing the Infinite

Stars unfold their silver grace,
Whispers of the cosmic dance,
In the void, a timeless space,
Every glance, a fleeting chance.

Galaxies swirl in a dream,
Wonders stretch beyond our sight,
Within the vast, endless seam,
We chase the echoes of light.

Hearts soar on celestial winds,
Boundless as the heavens wide,
In the night, our spirit spins,
Embracing all that's deep inside.

With each breath, the universe,
Fills our souls, ignites the spark,
A symphony, a gentle verse,
In the void, we leave our mark.

Hand in hand, we wander far,
Beneath the same infinite stars.

Melodies Beneath the Surface

Under waves, the secrets sing,
Tides whisper tales of the deep,
In currents, life finds its wing,
A world below where visions creep.

Coral gardens bloom and sway,
Fish flit in colors bright,
Each ripple and each ray,
Craft a song in liquid light.

Muffled rhythms of the sea,
Echo through the ocean swell,
In the depths, a symphony,
Where silence holds its breath swell.

Beneath the foam, the pulse beats,
Anchored in the ocean's heart,
Each moment, a dance completes,
As waves and melodies impart.

Listen close to water's tune,
In its depths, dreams find their bloom.

Celestial Embrace

Moonlight bathes the world in glow,
Soft shadows play on the ground,
In night's arms, the secrets flow,
In silence, we are wrapped, profound.

Stars alight with gentle grace,
Each twinkle speaks of ancient tales,
In the dark, our souls embrace,
We drift where living starlight sails.

In twilight's tender, sweet caress,
Dreams entwine in cosmic streams,
In the hush, we find our rest,
Where whispers weave of timeless dreams.

With every breath, we taste the void,
Infinite, we seek to trace,
In night's magic, love deployed,
Together, in this celestial space.

Embracing all that fills the skies,
We find our home in the night's guise.

A Canvas of Radiant Whispers

Colors dance in the morning light,
Gentle hues in a world so bright.
Brush strokes weave tales untold,
On canvas, dreams begin to unfold.

Nature's palette, bold and grand,
Whispers of peace from every land.
Each hue a story, each shade a song,
In this realm, I truly belong.

Clouds drift softly, gray to white,
Embracing the warmth, chasing the night.
The breeze carries secrets, soft and light,
In the canvas painted with pure delight.

Mountains stand tall, guardians wise,
Reflecting truths beneath their skies.
Rivers carve paths, timeless and free,
In every brush stroke, a symphony.

As sunlight wanes, colors fade,
Yet the memory of beauty stayed.
In the whispers of twilight's kiss,
Lies a promise of enduring bliss.

The Lullaby of the Horizon's Edge

Beneath the stars, the ocean sighs,
A serenade where silence flies.
Waves in rhythm, soft and slow,
A lullaby where dreams will flow.

The horizon glows with amber hues,
Whispers of night, in evening's muse.
Gentle breezes carry tales,
In this hush, the heart prevails.

Clouds embrace the fading light,
A canvas of day turning to night.
With every breath, the world finds peace,
In this moment, all worries cease.

Stars awaken in velvet skies,
Glistening gems, each one replies.
Stories shared from far and wide,
In the lullaby, we confide.

As twilight deepens, shadows creep,
In the stillness, secrets keep.
At horizon's edge, we softly tread,
To the melody where dreams are led.

Meditations on the Dusk's Lure

In the stillness of the fading day,
Dusk beckons me, urging to stay.
Shadows stretch as colors blend,
In this moment, time seems to bend.

The sky wears robes of crimson shade,
Painting visions that will not fade.
Whispers of twilight, soft and sweet,
Wrap the world in a gentle sheet.

Stars ignite in the evening's grace,
Guiding hearts to a sacred space.
In reflections of the night's embrace,
We find solace's tender trace.

Each breath a song, each sigh a prayer,
As dreams unfold in the cool night air.
Meditate on the dusk's sweet lure,
In its silence, we find the cure.

As night deepens, the world retreats,
In quiet corners, our spirit meets.
With every flicker of the stars so bright,
We dance in shadows, embracing the night.

Threads of Connection Through the Sky

Woven strands of the skyline's grace,
Bridges of light, a warm embrace.
In the tapestry where all align,
We find the threads that intertwine.

Clouds drift together, soft and white,
Creating paths in the fading light.
Each moment shared, a precious thread,
Connecting hearts wherever we tread.

The sun dips low, kissing the earth,
In this canvas, we find our worth.
Birds in flight paint arcs of gold,
Stories of love and journeys bold.

Moonlight bathes the world in dreams,
Painting life with silvery beams.
In the quiet, our souls explore,
Threads of connection, forevermore.

As night unfolds, stars start to gleam,
We weave our wishes into the stream.
With every twinkle, bonds arise,
Threads of connection through the skies.

Celestial Conversations at Dusk

As stars awaken in the night,
They whisper secrets, soft and bright.
The moon, a pearl in velvet skies,
Holds tales of old in silver sighs.

Each twinkle sparks a fleeting thought,
Of dreams once lost and battles fought.
In twilight's glow, all seems to blend,
A cosmic dance, where souls transcend.

The horizon blurs, where day meets night,
A place of peace, a soft delight.
Time whispers low, as shadows creep,
In cosmic chats, the heavens leap.

With every breath, the universe sings,
A harmony of forgotten things.
In dusk's embrace, we find our voice,
In celestial conversations, we rejoice.

So let us pause and lose the hour,
In gentle thoughts, we find our power.
For every star that lights the air,
Is part of us, beyond compare.

Dreaming in the Palette of Twilight

The sky transforms in hues so rare,
As twilight paints with gentle care.
Brushstrokes of orange, pink, and blue,
Awakening dreams, a vibrant hue.

Beneath this canvas, hearts take flight,
As shadows blend with fading light.
In every color, stories weave,
Echoes of what we dare believe.

Stars bloom softly, one by one,
Each a wish, a hope begun.
In the palette of this sacred hour,
We uncover depth in every flower.

As night creeps in, our dreams emerge,
In twilight's glow, our souls converge.
With every shade that starts to blend,
We find our truths, around the bend.

So linger longer, in this space,
Where colors mingle, hearts embrace.
In dreams of dusk, we softly soar,
Forever lost, yet seeking more.

In Search of the Whispering Winds

In fields of gold, the breezes play,
They weave through grasses, sway and sway.
A gentle touch, a tender call,
In whispers soft, they speak to all.

Through valleys deep and mountains high,
They carry tales that drift and fly.
In every gust, a story flows,
The secrets of the earth, it knows.

Among the trees, the voices rise,
A symphony beneath the skies.
Each leaf that rustles has a say,
In the dance of winds, we find our way.

With every breath, we lean in close,
To hear the dreams, the hope, the prose.
In search of wisdom, lost in time,
The whispering winds, a gentle rhyme.

So let us wander where they lead,
In nature's heart, we plant the seed.
For in the winds, our spirits lift,
A journey shared, life's precious gift.

Esoteric Rhythms of the Universe

In silence deep, the cosmos hums,
An ancient tune, where wisdom drums.
Every star, a pulse of grace,
In rhythms lost, we find our place.

Galaxies swirl in mystical dance,
A cosmic fate, a fleeting chance.
In quantum beats and silent waves,
The universe sings what time engraves.

Eclipses shadow, but light reveals,
A language felt, not one that heals.
With every cycle, life renews,
In esoteric paths, we choose.

From atoms small to worlds so vast,
The heartbeat echoes from the past.
In every moment, all is one,
In dance of shadows, light's begun.

So let us listen, embrace the sound,
In every heartbeat, we are found.
For in the cosmic, vibrant spins,
Lie rhythms pure, where life begins.

www.ingramcontent.com/pod-product-compliance
Ingram Content Group UK Ltd.
Pitfield, Milton Keynes, MK11 3LW, UK
UKHW021413220125
4239UKWH00007B/69